Now I See Why Life Is Like An Olympic Dream

Now I See Why Life Is Like An Olympic Dream
ISBN 0-88144-196-1

Application has been made for a registered federal trademark for "Rhymeo" and "Show-It Poet."

Copyright © 1996 Dan and Dave Davidson
Rhymeo Ink
P.O. Box 1416
Salem, VA 24153

Published by Trade Life
P.O. Box 55325
Tulsa, OK 74155

To my children Jacob, Noah & Kirsti
I'll always believe in you and your Olympic Dreams
With love from Dad
Dan Davidson

To my first son due this summer,
Welcome to the starting blocks of life
Dave Davidson

WHAT'S A RHYMEO™?

Rhymeos™ are fat-free un-poetry – lite and lean literary cuisine. Rhymeos™ are short and sketchy, quick and catchy – two short lines reinforced in rhyme. Although the short rhyming couplets display a poetic flavor, they are not traditional poetry. They are actually jingles about life – Jingle Verse Poetry for the 21st Century – offering insight and motivation, humor and inspiration.

Cyrano De Words-u-lac pens the shortest verse in the universe – a story to tell in a nutshell, a rhyming report to make a long story short. Rhymeos™ are short and sweet and poetically petite – clever ways to paraphrase – bite-sized words to the wise. Whether concise advice or an easy doesy fuzzy wuzzy, Rhymeos™ give a reflective perspective in a fireside chat format. It's literary rap with a snap – poetically correct dialect – a way to cope with humor and hope!

Applying The Ambition
Of Olympic Competition

Everyone has an Olympic dream to pursue
and each one deserves faithful follow through.
Even though they may not be part of the Games,
all our lifelong dreams are worthy just the same.

Some have let go of Olympic dreams in their heart,
while others move too slow or never even start.
But winners in life press on applying the ambition
found within the dream of Olympic competition.

Cyrano De Words-u-lac

OLYMPIC DREAM PERSISTENCE PLAN

Be BOLD
Think WOW with Olympic Dreams
Be SOLD
Make a VOW with Olympic Devotion
Make the MOLD
Plan HOW with Olympic Details
Go for GOLD
Do it NOW with Olympic Deeds
Never FOLD
Push the PLOW with Olympic Diligence

BE BOLD

Think Wow
Olympic Dreams

Aim high
do or die.

Dare to dream
to the extreme.

*Now I See Why
Life Is Like
An Olympic Dream;
Going For The Gold
Builds Self-Esteem.*

Fix your eyes on the prize.

Make it your aim to win the game.

Be bold
for the gold.

**Never stop
aiming for the top.**

**Don't let dreams drag
or do a zigzag.**

Now I See Why Life Is Like A Bow And Arrow; The Best Path Is Straight And Narrow.

**Always try
for a bullseye.**

**Dream like you are
an Olympic star.**

*Now I See Why
Life Is Like
A Yacht Or Boat;
Setting Your Sails
Keeps Dreams
Afloat.*

Make it essential to pursue potential.

Drive in the direction of personal perfection.

***D**on't ever spike
someone you
don't like.*

Keep warm
to stay in good form.

Have nutrition
intuition.

*Now I See Why
Life Is Like
A Pitcher's Mound;
Aiming Is Better
On Higher Ground.*

**Don't be intimidated
by opponents overrated.**

**Live up to your dream;
don't give up on your team.**

*Now I See Why
Life Is Like
A Good Attitude;
Success Can
Depend On How
Life Is Viewed.*

**Strive and seek
to reach your peak.**

**Be a go-getter,
never a quitter.**

Now I See Why
Life Is Like
A Balance Beam;
Walking The Line
Helps Fulfill
A Dream.

**Keep hope in mind
when running behind.**

**Be an all-around winner
like Bruce Jenner.**

BE SOLD

Make A Vow
Olympic Devotion

**Commmit your heart
before you start.**

**Have an over-the-fence
self confidence.**

Now I See Why Life Is Like A Sharpshooter's Scope; Without A Vision Goals Lack Hope.

Take an oath
for personal growth.

Prevent the event
of discouragement.

It's not whether you win or lose, but the attitude you choose.

Focus vision with precision.

Display dedication for the duration.

*Now I See Why
Life Is Like
A Free Throw;
Even A Sure Shot
Can Be A No-Go.*

Train toward reaping a reward.

Keep your pride in proper stride.

Apply the ambition of Olympic competition.

Get a good grip on sportsmanship.

Be a good loser, not an excuser.

Now I See Why Life Is Like Team Participation; Playing In The Games Benefits Your Nation.

**Instill within
the will to win.**

**Pay the price
of sacrifice.**

Now I See Why Life Is Like Showing Respect; Honoring Others Has A Ripple Effect.

Have a higher desire as in *Chariots of Fire*.

Now I See Why Life Is Like A Hockey Puck; Making A Goal Takes More Than Luck.

Concentrate at the plate.

Always insist on being an optimist.

Now I See Why
Life Is Like
The Olympic Rings;
Colors Coming
Together Is What
Unity Brings.

Be a better pacesetter.

Use your head to win time and again.

Now I See Why Life Is Like A Diving Board; A Good Send-Off Reaps A Reward.

Congratulate winners, gold medalists and beginners.

Shake off the jinx if your play sinks.

Never kick an ump in the rump.

Never fret
at the net.

Don't be a complainer
to a coach or a trainer.

Now I See Why Life Is Like Being An Athlete; There's Thrill In Victory And Agony In Defeat.

Be a master
of learning faster.

Keep your strive
always alive.

*Now I See Why
Life Is Like
A Slam At The Net;
Half Of The Game
Is Mental Mindset.*

As a rule
keep your cool.

*Now I See Why
Life Is Like
A Flying Javelin;
You Can Go Far
In Life If Dared
To Be Driven.*

Train
to remain.

Relay the rationale
to boost morale.

Now I See Why Life Is Like A Standing Ovation; There's A Time To Join In A Celebration.

Beat the rest to be the best.

Don't wait too late to accelerate.

Now I See Why
Life Is Like
A Long Jump Leap;
For Dreams To Soar
Hope Needs
Upkeep.

Cheer and support your team on the court.

MAKE THE MOLD

Plan How
Olympic Details

Have a game plan to be the best you can.

Design a grand how-to plan.

*N*ow I See Why
Life Is Like
An Umpire's Call;
A Just Judge
Is Best For All.

**Be humble
if you stumble.**

**Never boast
or coast.**

Now I See Why
Life Is Like
A Relay Race;
It Takes Teamwork
To Finish First
Place.

To be number one don't jump the gun.

Know when to tread and when to go ahead.

Be a good sport and always exhort.

Don't commit beyond your limit.

Never choose to lose.

Now I See Why Life Is Like A Volleyball Spike; An Unselfish Assist Sets Up A Strike.

Be right on passing the baton.

Never swear after an error.

Now I See Why Life Is Like A Boxing Ring; Corners Are Good For Regrouping.

Prepare with flair.

Think in sync.

Play fair and square.

Hour by hour, train with will power.

Practice and prep to stay in step.

Now I See Why
Life Is Like
A Time Trial;
A Good Showing
Proves Practice
Is Worthwhile.

Never cheat when you compete.

Drive to win with discipline.

**On your mark,
get set, go,
be the spark
of the show.**

Don't complain about the game.

Never bellyache over a mistake.

*Now I See Why
Life Is Like
A Foul Line;
Boundaries Exist
By Divine Design.*

**Build and esteem
the rest of your team.**

**As a ref or judge
be slow to budge.**

Now I See Why Life Is Like A Cycling Course; Country Roads Reveal Creation's Source.

Don't follow the forecast that nice guys finish last.

Now I See Why Life Is Like Olympic Flames; We All Share The Spirit Behind The Games.

Plan and prepare to practice with care.

Don't let losing a race be a training waste.

GO FOR GOLD

Do It Now
Olympic Deeds

Try to be
an M.V.P.

Start somehow
to do it now.

Now I See Why Life Is Like A Starting Block; A Good Beginning Helps Beat The Clock.

Never flunk
a slam dunk.

Give each shot
all you've got.

Now I See Why
Life Is Like
Going For Gold;
Winning Can
Take Effort A
Hundred Fold.

Minimize the "butterflies."

Make the move to improve.

Now I See Why Life Is Like An Opening Ceremony; Nations Coming Together Can Be A Testimony.

Get-up-and-go like a dynamo.

Rise to the occasion with determination.

Never hurdle like a turtle.

**Take the lead
with skill and speed.**

**Be quick on your feet
and don't be beat.**

Now I See Why Life Is Like A World Record; The Best Often Have The Last Word.

**Take first place
with style and grace.**

**When diving a lot,
double tie your suit not.**

Now I See Why
Life Is Like
A Gold Medal;
To Be The Best
You Can't
Backpedal.

Try harder to be a self-starter.

Pass the test to be the best.

Don't be beat
in a dead heat.

Don't be a grump when in a slump.

Do the dash in a flash.

Now I See Why Life Is Like A Performance; Giving Your Best Leads To Excellence.

Be as quick as you can as a relay anchor man.

Be stronger longer.

Add perspiration to your aspiration.

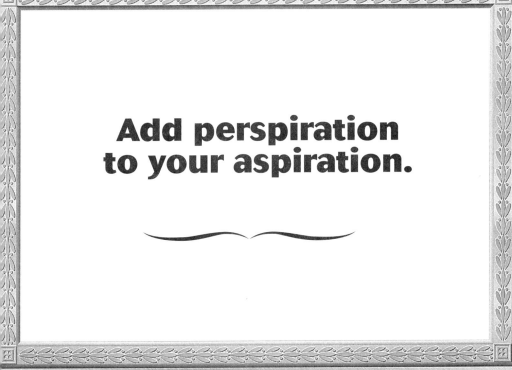

Dodge the defense with common sense.

Take the hint to sprint.

Now I See Why Life Is Like The 100m Dash; Opportunity Can Come And Go In A Flash.

**Don't ever miss
a chance for an assist.**

**Keep the lead
to succeed.**

Now I See Why Life Is Like Water Polo; A Team Can Sink If Someone Goes Solo.

**Start with a sprint
in your main event.**

**Have the touch
in the clutch.**

Perform to win with a perfect ten.

**Don't go
with a low blow.**

**Give extra umph
for a triumph.**

Now I See Why Life Is Like Skating On Thin Ice; Warning Signs Are Good Advice.

Always wish for a swish.

Take time to train in sunshine or rain.

Now I See Why Life Is Like A Bobsled Ride; On Life's Fast Track We Need A Guide.

**Make history
with a victory.**

**Capture the crown
hands down.**

*Now I See Why
Life Is Like
A Soccer Kick;
Goals Are Made
With Moves That
Are Quick.*

**Keep wasted seconds
fewest
like speedster
Carl Lewis.**

NEVER FOLD

Push The Plow
Olympic Diligence

Daily be diligent and persistent.

If at first you don't succeed, persevere and proceed.

Now Is See Why
Life Is Like
A Canoe Paddle;
Persistent Pursuit
Can Help Win
A Battle.

If knocked down, get up off the ground.

Don't be the sort to fall short.

*Now I See Why
Life Is Like
A Marathon;
It Keeps Going
On And On And On.*

Never hit the deck when it's neck and neck.

Stay in it to win it.

Now I See Why Life Is Like A Pole Vault; Challenges Should Be Approached With Assault.

Keep pace in life's race.

Go over, around or through obstacles in front of you.

Now I See Why
Life Is Like
A Speed Skater;
With Quick
Precision
Success Is Greater.

Don't pout after a strikeout.

Always endure after failure.

Now I See Why Life Is Like A Shot Put Throw; Burdens Surrendered Can Help Us Grow.

Don't diminish
at a photo finish.

Know winners never quit
and quitters never get it.

Be a marathon phenomenon.

**Improve your hustle
and move more muscle.**

**Develop the discipline
of not giving up or in.**

Now I See Why Life Is Like Cross Country Skis; A Long Journey Isn't A Breeze.

Lower resistance and go the distance.

Stamp out doubt.

*Now I See Why
Life Is Like
A Ski Jump;
A Lift Can Get You
Over The Hump.*

**Build up momentum
for a winning outcome.**

**Like Edwin Moses soar
for another encore.**

*Now I See Why
Life Is Like
The Steeplechase;
Hurdles Can
Hinder The Pace
Of A Race.*

Increase will
when going uphill.

Stay on track
for a comeback.

Be confident and diligent and give 110 percent.

**Never quit
staying fit.**

**Keep in mind
the finish line.**

Now I See Why Life Is Like A Shot At The Buzzer; When Time Is Short Don't Go Easy Does-er.

Don't go weak during a hot streak.

If at first you don't win, try, try again.

Now I See Why Life Is Like A 40-Love Score; To Come Back You Have To Want It More.

Be one
to overcome.

Develop assurance
with endurance.

Now I See Why Life Is Like A Second Wind; Extra Strength Comes From Discipline.

**Be ready
and stay steady.**

**Be humble in case
you come in second place.**

Join the celebration of a standing ovation.

Don't rub it in when you win.

Display desire down to the wire.

Now I See Why Life Is Like Worthy Opponents; Competition Can Bring Out Excellence.

Go for your goal
with heart, mind and soul.

Like Wilma Rudolph
overcome
what others say
can't be done.

Now I See Why Life Is Like Skiing Downhill; Challenging Dreams Are A Thrill To Fulfill.

Stretch to surpass as the best in your class.

Don't just compare from the armchair.

Now I See Why Life Is Like Persistent Practice; Becoming A Winner Isn't Hit Or Miss.

**Plan to persist
hand over fist.**

**Go the extra mile
during a time trial.**

Never look back leading the pack.

Go against trends like Jesse Owens.

Return and rebound when you're down.

Now I See Why Life Is Like The Decathlon; A Versatile Player Is One To Depend On.

Gain an edge
with a persistence pledge.

Olympic Edge
Persistence Pledge:

**I am willing to be rejected or fail up to
1,000 times before I prevail.**

*Now I See Why
Life Is Like
A Finish Line;
There Comes
A Time In
The End To Shine.*

A TALE TO KNOW BY CYRANO

The Inspiration Behind A Legend In His Own Rhyme
Let me share with you a tale of inspiration and betrayal,
a story of poetic word, of my great,
great granddad Cyrano de Bergerac.
For he had a tender heart and his nose was a work of art,
as a poet the part he played was that
of a romantic serenade.
While another man spoke his prose,
granddad hid behind his nose,
as the maiden was swayed by the rhyme
of his friend's charade.
Generations later I found out about this hoax
behind his snout,
and as a youth I felt betrayed by his phony masquerade.
I became ashamed of this mimicry
and the heritage of my family,

but then one day I read by chance,
the words he used for romance.
It was then when my heart realized the legacy
of my family ties.
I saw him in a new light. My heart was touched,
and now I write.
The prose composed from my pen,
I propose as a new trend . . .
poetic proverbs known as *Rhymeos*™,
by the Show-It Poet™ Cyrano,
Rearranged along this path of fame,
was my granddad's last name,
no longer am I called de Bergerac;
I am *Cyrano De Words-u-lac.*
If you find your lines are few, the words
you lack I'll choose for you.
For I've pledged to become over time . . .
a legend in my own rhyme.

WHO IS CYRANO?

a literary dignitary
a word weaver
Rhymeo™ retriever
a prolific writer
and poetic reciter
among supermen
of the fountain pen
Cyrano De Words-u-lac
is the combined pen name of brothers
Dr. Dan the Man and Dave the Wave Davidson

PARTNERS IN RHYME

the brothers behind Cyrano's mind
As legend has it, this modern day Show-It Poet™
is the great, great, grandson of the literary figure
Cyrano de Bergerac.

More Rhymeo™ Titles
by Cyrano De Words-u-lac

Diamond Dreams

If I Could Live My Life Again. . .

A Mother's Love Is Made Up Of . . .

Home & Heart Improvement For Men

It's Time Again To Skip A Birthday When . . .

**For more info and a FREE
Quill Guild™ Rhymeo™ newsletter**
Rhymeo Ink   P. O. Box 1416   Salem, VA 24153
phone (540) 989-0592   1 - 8 0 0 - 4 - R H y M E O
http://www.rhymeo.com   rhymeo@aol.com